GRANT THE GRAPEFRUIT TOURS NEW ZEALAND

Samantha Key

ISBN: 1537073680
ISBN-13: 978-1537073682

To my friends and family who have encouraged me to fulfil my dreams.

IN THE BEGINNING

This book tells the true story of Grant the Grapefruit and how his life was dramatically changed from one of predictability and certainty to one of adventure.

So let us begin....

Once upon a time (all good stories start like this) in a land far, far away grew a grapefruit tree in a garden of a house. One warm Autumn day, a visitor from a far-away land called the United Kingdom came for a short stay at the house. The visitor was amazed that her favourite fruit was growing so abundantly on the large tree in the garden. She had never seen a grapefruit tree before, as where she lived they did not grow very easily. As a gift, a small grapefruit was given to the visitor from the tree. In order to make the grapefruit extra special a face was drawn on the grapefruit. This is how Grant the grapefruit's adventures started, how he got his name and this book will help you discover why he has a smile on his face.

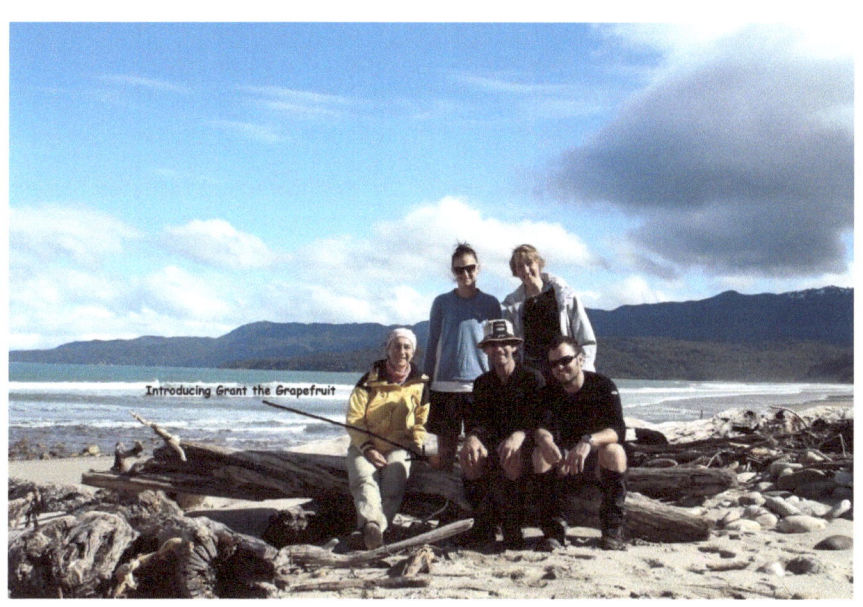

Introducing Grant the Grapefruit

That mountain top feeling

Our brave grapefruit's adventure starts a little differently to what you may have imagined. He is completely in the dark. He knows that something different, new and exciting is about to happen but he is not sure exactly what. Little did Grant realise that this is mainly because he is in the middle of a rucksack, which would probably feel the same as being hidden under a blanket. He cannot see anything and is relying on his other senses to provide him with information about the outside world.

Once the gentle rhythmic swaying has subsided he feels himself being uncomfortably jolted around. Grant is blissfully unaware of the encounters which his carrier is facing, such as getting stuck on trees which have fallen and covered a small mountain track. Most of the trekkers on the journey had decided to climb under the trees. Grant's adventurous owner decides that she can make it over them instead. The first one is tackled in this manner without any problems. The second tree is slightly wider and, having misjudged the distance and width of the tree trunk, she finds herself straddled across it like she is riding a horse, with neither feet touching the ground and clinging on for dear life whilst trying not to look down and panic.

Grant begins to feel the temperature getting cooler and his first glimpse of daylight is at the top of an amazing mountain, Key Summit, which is in Fiordland National Park. He is placed on an icy cold metal circle which quickly jolts him awake. He soon forgets the unpleasant feeling of the cold creeping through his peel as he is begins to take in the beautiful panoramic view.

This is how all good journey's start, completely in the dark, unsure of your direction but with a feeling and a knowing that you are about to begin something amazing which will change your life, and how you view it forever. You may have some feelings of apprehension, these are muffled by the intense feelings of excitement. Some people would call these feelings fear, but if you compare the two feelings, fear and excitement, you will find that they are not so different. The difference between them is how you decide to interpret them. Do you live in fear of life and all it has to offer, in fear of change? Or do you choose to be excited by the unknown and the new? The choice is yours. One direction will lead you to experience life in all it's glory, the other will lead to a world which is small and safe.

For our friend Grant, he decided to choose to feel excitement and the reward which he received for this decision only just beginning.

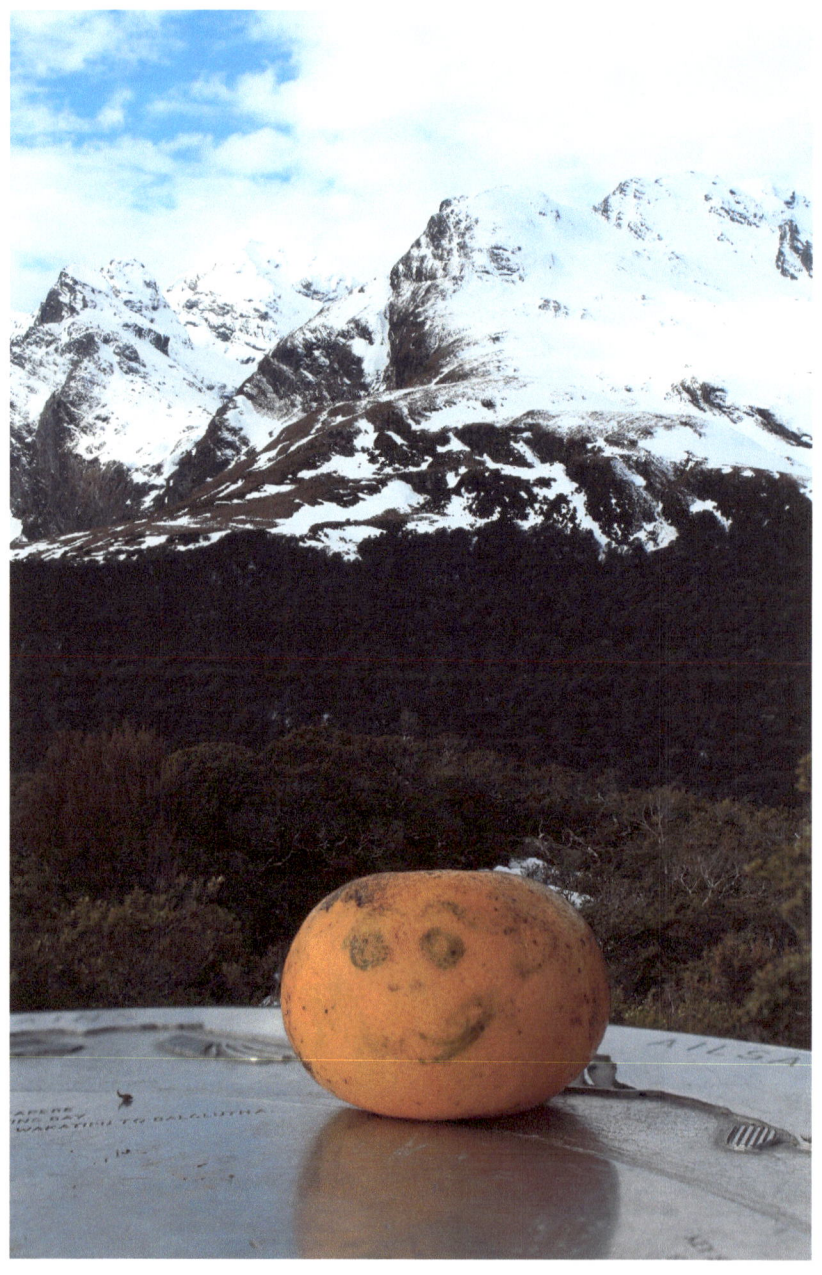

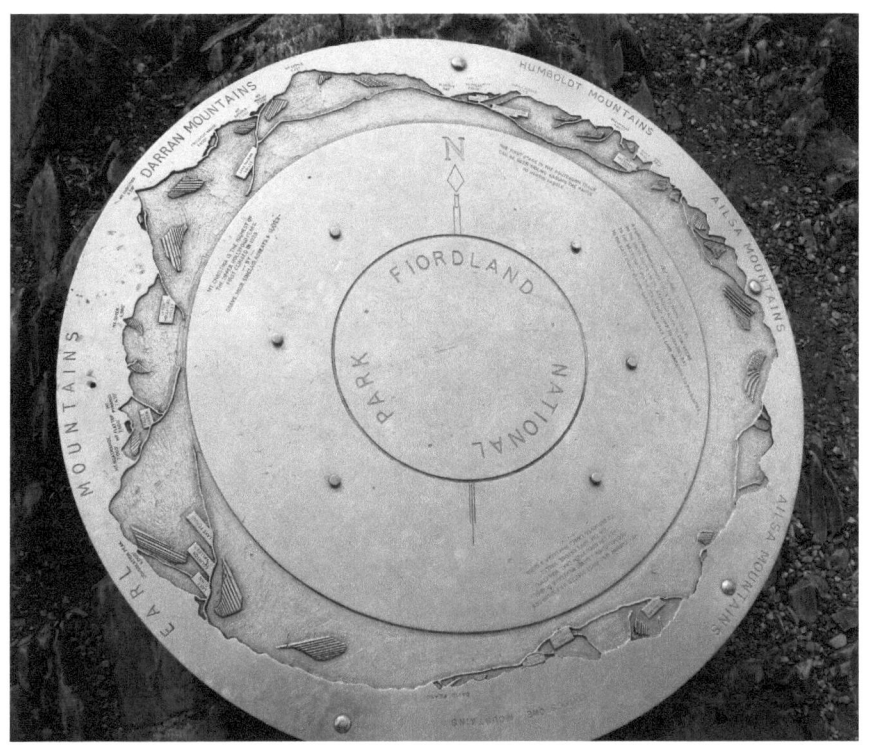

Milford Sound

Our intrepid, brave grapefruit has just conquered his first mountain. It feels like a fantastic achievement. Little did he know that this was the first of many hurdles he was to overcome. When you set out to do anything new, to change something or go on an adventure no matter how detailed you plan it you are never 100% sure where you are going or where you will ultimately end up. You are entering uncharted territory which is usually outside of your understanding, experience and comfort zone. How can you plan for it if you don't know what it is? Each new adventure is like a warm up exercise, like an athlete stretching their muscles and mentally preparing themselves, and then you are off.

With each new adventure comes a new set of questions. Adding to your existing knowledge, like a computer adding to it's memory banks. When we experience something new, it can sometimes completely change the way we see the world. Grant's next life question to answer was: Do grapefruit's float?

Grant found himself in a bag again. This time there was something very different about this bag. Through the bag he can see a lovely yellow haze and he feels a gentle rocking sensation. He can hear the gentle swish of a paddle rhythmically hitting the water and the waves lapping at the side of a plastic canoe. When the bag is opened and lunch is taken out he is awestruck at what he can see. He is in the middle a wide expanse of water, with mountains towering on either side. He can hear the whoosh of a waterfall not too far off and the gentle lapping of shallow waves on the side of the plastic canoe. Grant is floating in the middle of the Milford Sound and the view from the water is spectacular!

This was the rest before the next part of his adventures, the relaxing part where everything goes still and quiet. He was on a mission to find the grapefruit within. The sense of calm and peace had overtaken any fears of whether or not he could float if the boat was to be rocked too far. On seeing the seals, who also seemed to be feeling the calm of the Milford Sound and at peace, he did begin to wonder, do seal's eat grapefruit?

As the questions swam around Grant's mind like the current around the canoe they began to spiral into a sensation of panic. Grant stopped himself and took a deep breath, observing that sometimes in life we can ask too many questions which get in the way of just enjoying the moment. The questions of anxiety drown out the intuitive voice within, like a white noise. Always there, constant and humming in the background. My questions come from my fear, realised Grant. Taking a deep breath, Grant bravely opened his eyes, which he hadn't even realised he had closed and once again he was amazed at the view which surrounded him.

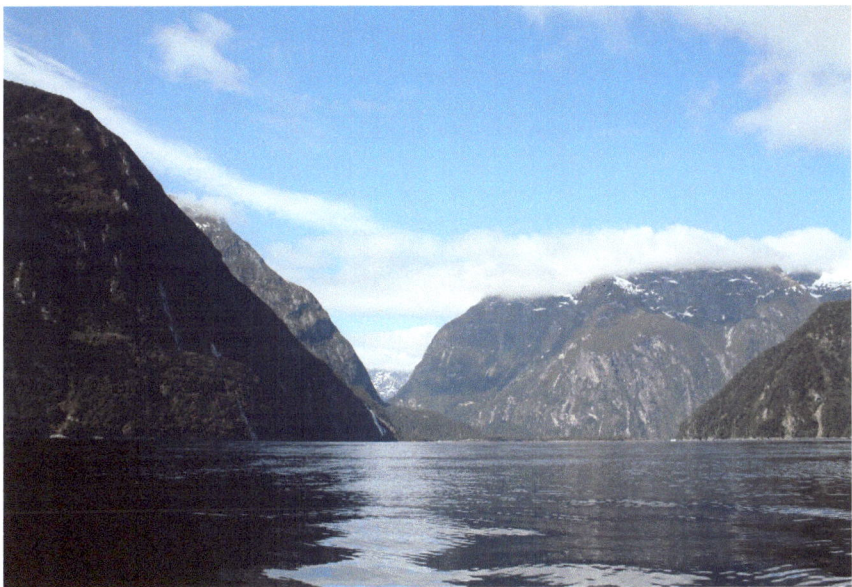

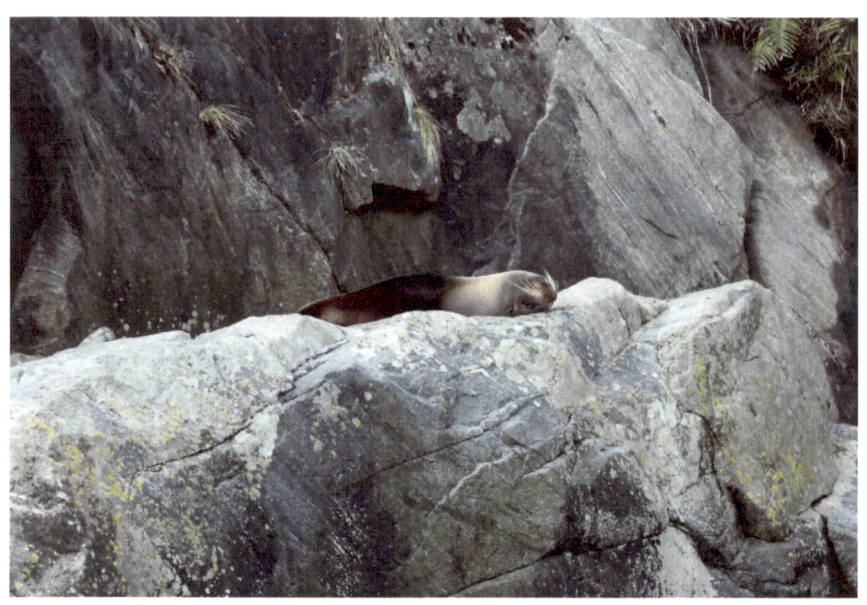

With a little help from my friends

Grant the Grapefruit, had enjoyed his canoe trip on the Milford Sound. What he was not aware of was that his biggest challenges were yet to come. Sometimes it is best not to know too much about your future. If we all knew what was to happen to us in life then we would probably choose to avoid things which would involve us facing our fears. In facing our fears we can feel the most amazing sense of achievement. It makes us stronger, more confident and makes us feel alive!

Grant had always had a fear of heights, being round he knew that in most situations he would roll to safety. However, most of the time when we are faced with our fears logical thinking like this goes right out of our heads. This is exactly what was happening to Grant at this moment in time.

The next day after his relaxing trip on the Milford Sound, Grant was faced with his fear of heights. There were several one man rope bridges to cross. These flimsy looking wooden and rope structures did not add to Grants confidence when he first saw them. They wobbled and creaked and groaned in protest with every step. What was worse is that they seemed to be getting higher and longer the further he went.

Thankfully, his first challenge was faced with the help of a friend. On every journey you make a friend. Sometimes they stay with you for a long time, sometimes it is to walk beside you for a few days. It does not matter how long they are with you. You are both on a shared adventure and journey, and both helping the other out along the way.

Our friends are our greatest gifts in life. If you have a friend who is prepared to stand by you through life's challenges then you have a rare gift indeed. This friend had walked this route many times before and their steady and persistent confidence enabled Grant to relax more. Just knowing that his new friend was there for him, no matter what or how silly he felt, gave Grant the strength to face anything and do everything that came his way that day. Grant had never had a friend before, but then he had never left the safety of his grapefruit tree.

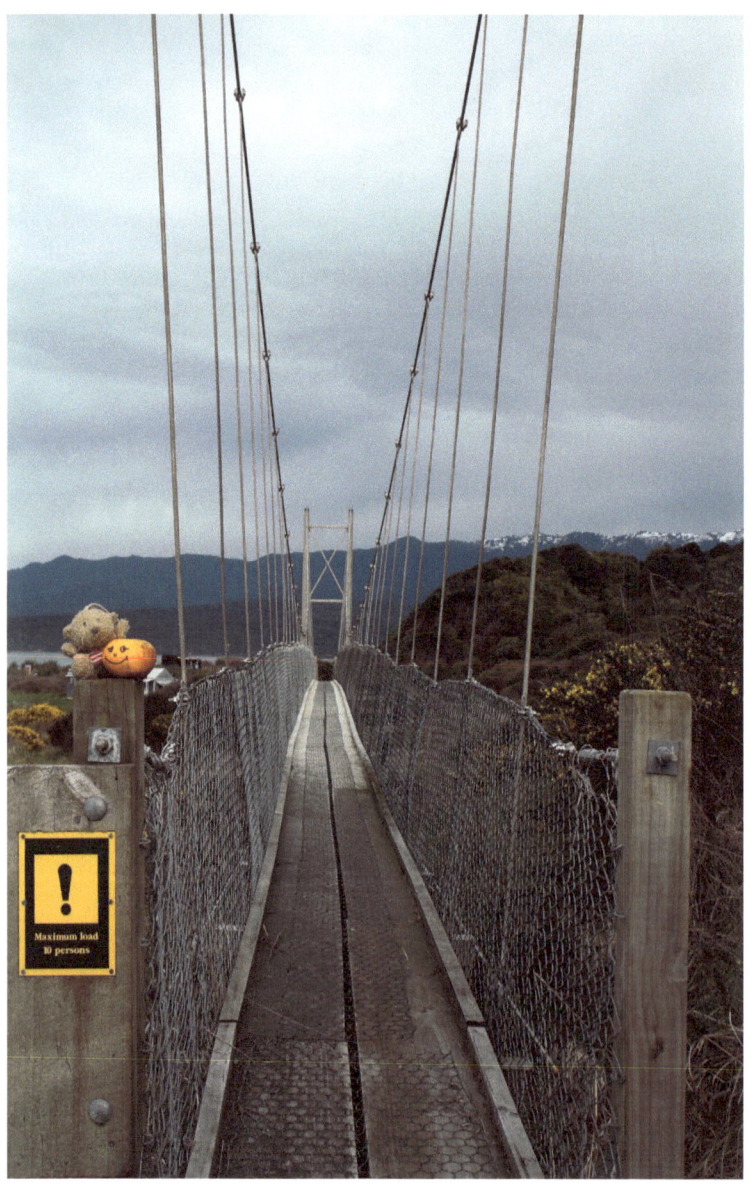

Embrace the journey

Have you ever had one of those days where you just want to hide? Well Grant was having one of those days!

Grant had spent the last few days facing his fear of water, fear of being eaten and his fear of heights. He was worn out! Grant was stronger than he ever thought he could be. It was at this moment Grant had two choices, he could hide away and wish he was back in his grapefruit tree, or he could push himself and see what this new day had in store for him.

While Grant was in the warm dark back pack he was in his bubble of safety. Most people have a bubble of safety. This is where you feel the most confident and comfortable. You know where the edges of your bubble are because you feel panic set in when they get too close to them. In the past few days Grant had bravely pushed the bubble and made his comfort zone bigger and stronger than before. He now know he could cope with being on a boat and he could roll across rope bridges.

If you look closely at the photograph and place where our grapefruit has decided to hide, is it really the safest place to be?

From Grant's hiding place he could see his new friends having so much fun. He began to feel left out and eventually he pushed his way through his mood and decided to join in with the laughter and fun. When he looked back at the place he had been hiding, he realised it was a huge water wheel and it probably wasn't the safe resting place he thought it was. Grant had just learnt to step back from his thoughts and have a look around at the bigger picture. This was to be a worthwhile lesson for the rest of his adventures.

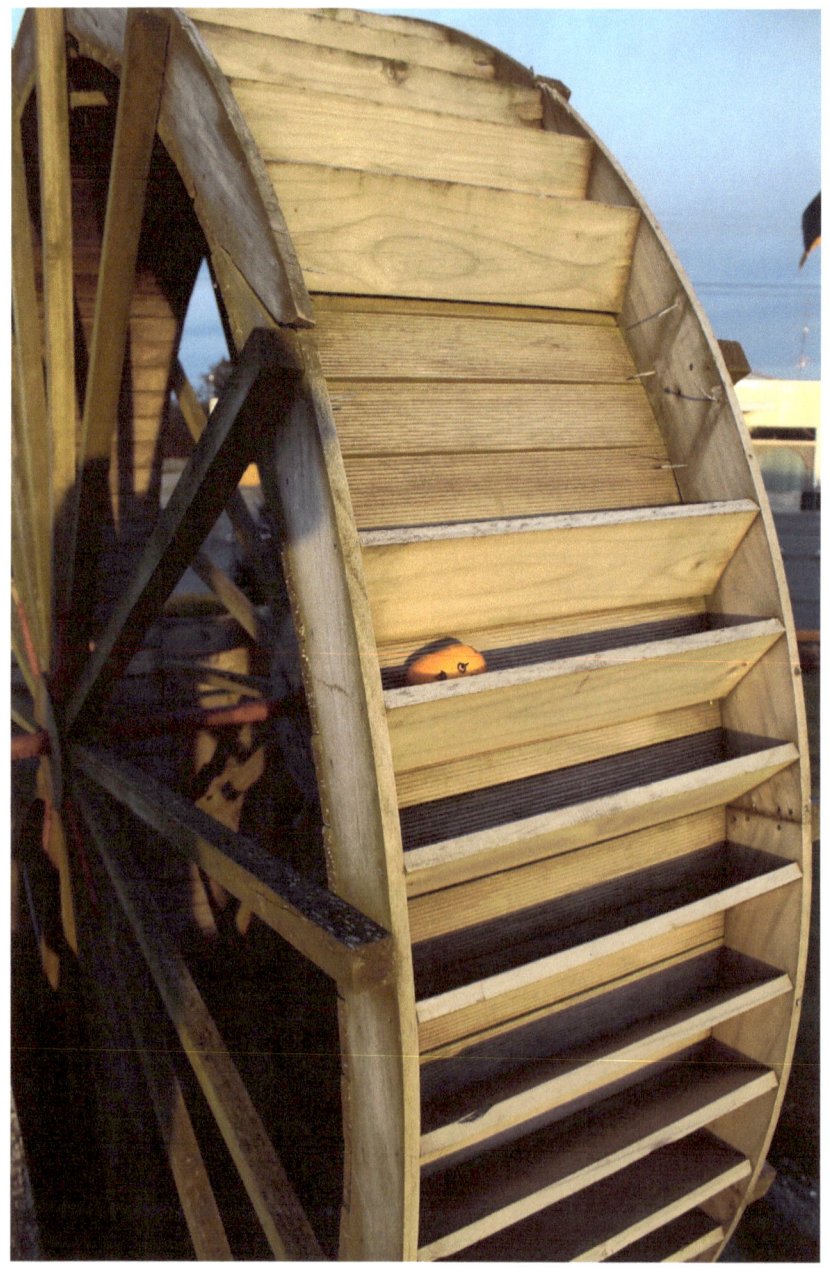

Communication

Another two day hike for our adventurous Grant was just beginning. The hike would take him along the Hunter Range and to Green Lake Hut. Thankfully Grant's only job was to not get jolted out of the back pack and they trundled along.

Being a grapefruit Grant had found it hard to tell his fellow travellers how he was feeling. He had never had to do this before, so it was completely new to him. Since the short space of time he had left the safety and comfort of his tree, Grant had felt excitement, fear, apprehension, joy and happiness. These were the emotions he knew about! He was pretty tired out from all the feelings he was having and appreciated the time he had now to watch and listen to his fellow travelling companions.

Grant decided that the best way to understanding people was to first listen to what they were saying. Being a grapefruit listening came quite easily to him. He had begun to notice that most people find listening a skill which is hard to master. They would much rather talk!

When you listen to someone you can work out what they are trying to say. You can ask questions to help you understand more. Grant was beginning to realise, the more he listened to others, the more they listened to him too. A conversation is a two way process. Grant was learning lots from listening to his travelling companions. He began to feel glad to be a grapefruit as being a human sounded like a lot of hard work!

As Grant bounced around in his backpack, which was now beginning to feel like home, he also realised that for the first time in his life he had friends. Grant had never thought about being lonely, until he realised what he had been missing and a sense of peace and happiness started to fill his grapefruit segments. He began to smile!

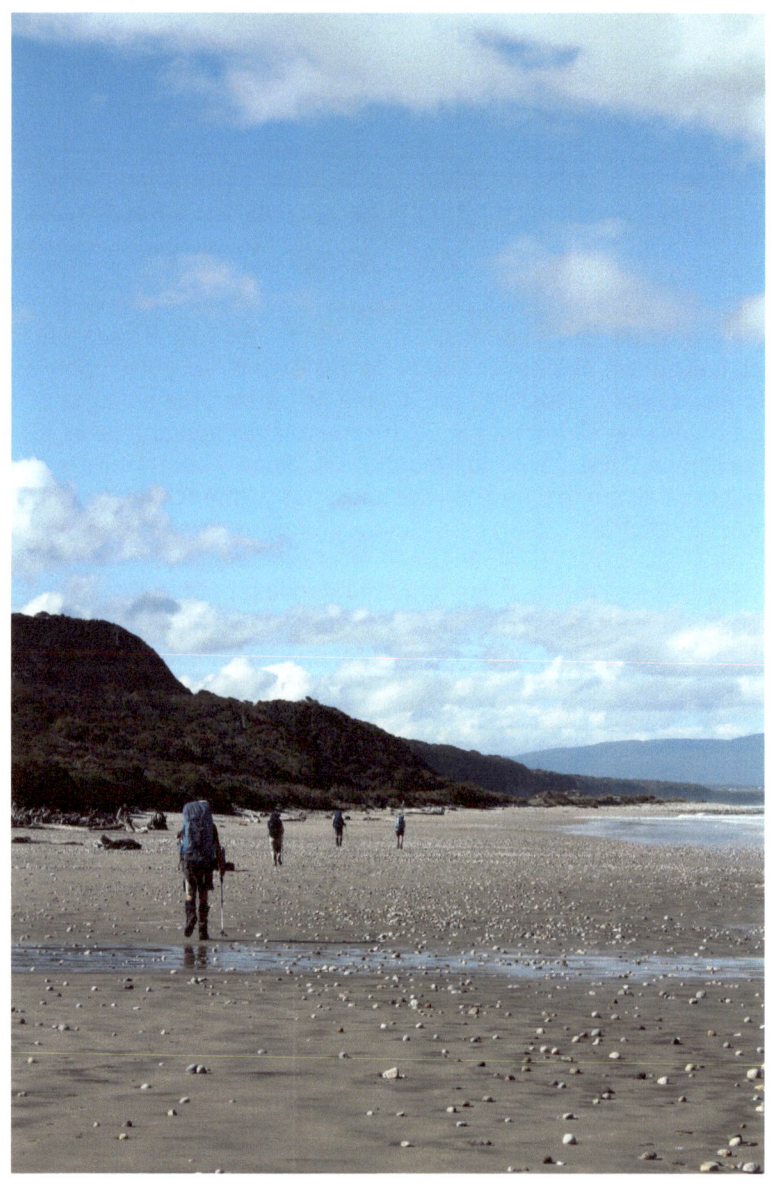

The steep climb to success

Grant was feeling that his adventures just kept getting bigger and bigger. When we last left our grapefruit friend he was contemplating his friends and how he had been learning to communicate with them better. He was beginning to realise that life is actually a bit like a rollercoaster, full of ups and downs, stops and starts. Sometimes he felt like he was screaming along at a rapid rate on his adventure and he did not have time to think about what he was doing he just had to do it.

Between these rapid rides he also found that he had some time for contemplation and thinking. He liked these times. It usually meant that there was a break in the challenges he was facing and he could have a good think about everything which he had just experienced. Grant realised he didn't have to sit and think, he could stay busy, but he quite liked these moments and felt they let everything sink into every segment of his being.

Grant was beginning to realise that he might not be in charge of what was going to happen next but he was in charge of how he reacted to it. A positive thought made the challenge so much more achievable. Rather than focusing on what he couldn't do and what he was scared of, with each little challenge he over came he was beginning to feel more positive about the next one that came along. He began to think "I can do this!" rather than "Oh no help!" and the more he did the more it was opening a whole new world to our little grapefruit.

Grant's next challenge was a test on everything he had learnt so far. Grant's seven hour hike lead him to the Percy Burn Viaduct....and his biggest challenge yet! His fear of falling was about to be tested as he bravely faced the 35 metre high viaduct. Looking down from the edge of the viaduct Grant felt slightly dizzy and wished he had hands so he could grip the edge of the viaduct tighter. One wrong roll and....gulp! He did not want to think about it.

Grant saw his colleagues walking across the bridge. He shut his eyes, rolled a little closer to the edge, reminded himself he could do this and started on the journey across the long viaduct pausing only one in the middle to take a peek down. He was surprised at how quickly he made it across the whole 125 meters to the other side of the bridge. He then discovered that there was a slippery journey down through the thick forest and undergrowth to the beach below. Again, he told himself he could do this and slowly rolled his way carefully down the embankment to the beach below.

Thinking that was the end of the challenge for the day Grant relaxed and took a moment to think about his achievement that day on the beautiful beach. It was then he realised that he would have to return to the top of the steep slopes before he could make his way back to the toasty warm cabin. This thought left him shaking in his peel. He froze and panicked and refused to move before he realised he was going to have to do this. He took a deep breath and began to make his way slowly up the steep slope at the side of the embankment. He decided he was not going to look back he was only going to look forwards.

Grant could not believe it when he finally reached the top he celebrated in style by leaping (possibly not voluntarily) from fellow trek members before being settled firmly back in the safety of his backpack to contemplate the achievement and challenges of the day.

The moral here? Well if a grapefruit can set his mind to it and achieve the impossible with a bit of positive thinking and determination, then so can anyone.

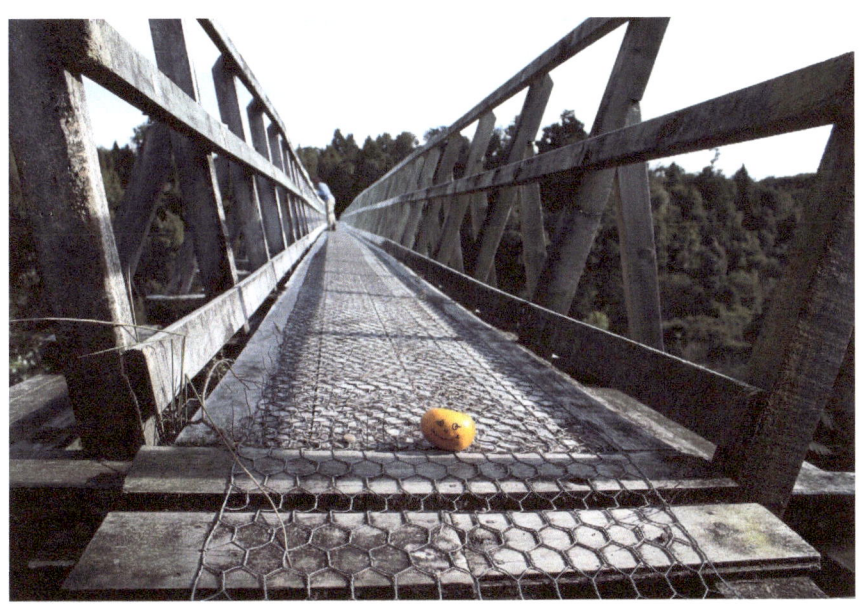

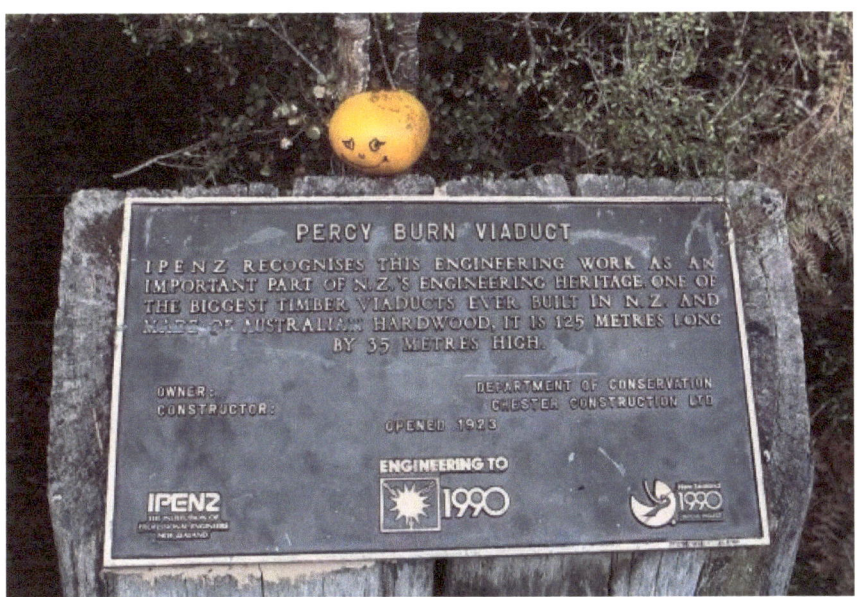

A feast with friends

Grant had learnt many things on his great grapefruit adventure. His next lesson was to learn that sometimes achievements can be recognised and celebrated by gathering friends for good food and an evening of laughter together. He had never had a reason to celebrate with friends as the grapefruits he knew were always on the same tree, in the same place, doing the same thing every since day. If you fell from the tree it was celebrated as a change but often you didn't get much further than sitting on the ground underneath the same place you had been looking at for your entire life.

The trek group Grant was with were making a Hangi feast. This is a traditional Maori way of cooking food and it involved a lot of team work. First the team dug a huge hole in the ground. Grant had a lack of limbs to hold the shovel so he was not very good at this bit. He helped by staying out of the way. Grant was very good at watching and listening. He was beginning to realised that that some people in the group were good at things the others were not. Together, as a team, they made a whole.

The next step in the process was to fill the hole with warm rocks from the fire. Again this was something which Grant was not very good at. He was also a little worried, being rock shaped himself, that he might be mistaken for a hot rock and placed in the pit.

Next, the food to be cooked was wrapped in foil and placed on top of the warm rocks in the hole. It was a bit like a layer cake but with dirt and rocks, thought Grant.

Finally, the soil which was removed to make the hole is used to cover the food and a fire is lit on the top. This is where Grant's skills came into their own. Being round he found he could easily roll over the dirt and flatten it ready for the next layer to be placed on.

The feast took two hours to cook. This gave the whole group time to explore the deserted beaches and watch the amazing multicoloured sunset with a group of fur seals close by.

Little did Grant know that this was just the start of an amazing evening.

As the stars came out in the clear night sky, Grant rolled onto his back to admire them while listening to the stories and discussions that were taking place around the campsite. Grant was beginning to realise that it is also a wonderful feeling to be completely in the present moment.

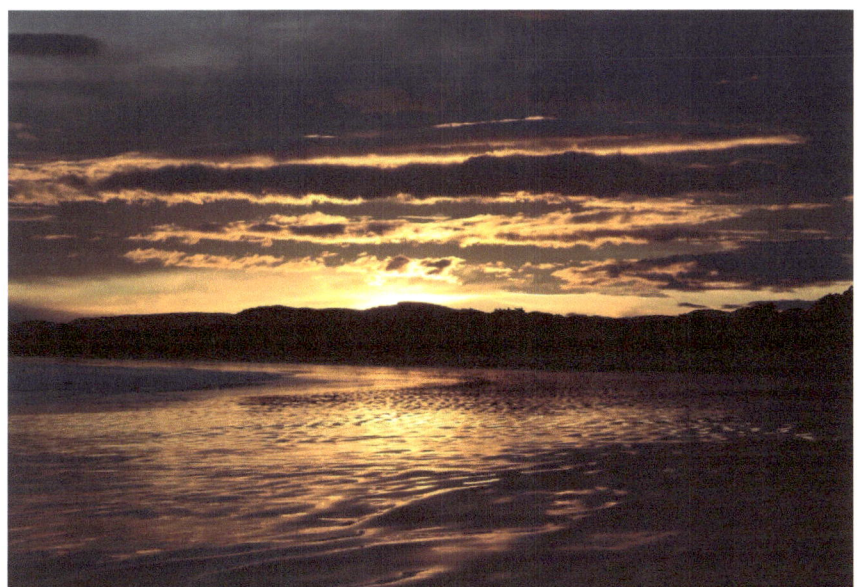

Bliss

There are some moments that make you realise that life is really a truly magical experience. I am sure that you have heard the phrase the calm before the storm? Well for Grant the Grapefruit the next step on his adventure was to be more like the calm in the eye of the storm. This is where everything is happening around you but you remain in perfect harmony and balance completely obvious to it all. This moment was to be more life transforming that any other moment Grant had experienced on his adventure so far.

So far Grant has had a lot of new and exciting experiences. One adventure after another has put some stress on his little segments.

Feeling tired and weary Grant was removed from his back pack and found himself in a run down house. It was simple, no fancy dressings but the view from the battered bedroom balcony was absolute bliss! A curving beach, with gently rolling waves lapping the sands, no sound, a warm soft breeze and the opportunity to see dolphins playing joyously in the surf. What more could a Grapefruit ask for? As Grant sat on the balcony admiring the view and soaking up the atmosphere for the first time in his short existence he felt a strange inner feeling of complete calm and bliss. It was truly magical! He decided that he wanted this moment to never end and drifted into a half awake, half asleep slumber which his aching segments quite desperately needed.

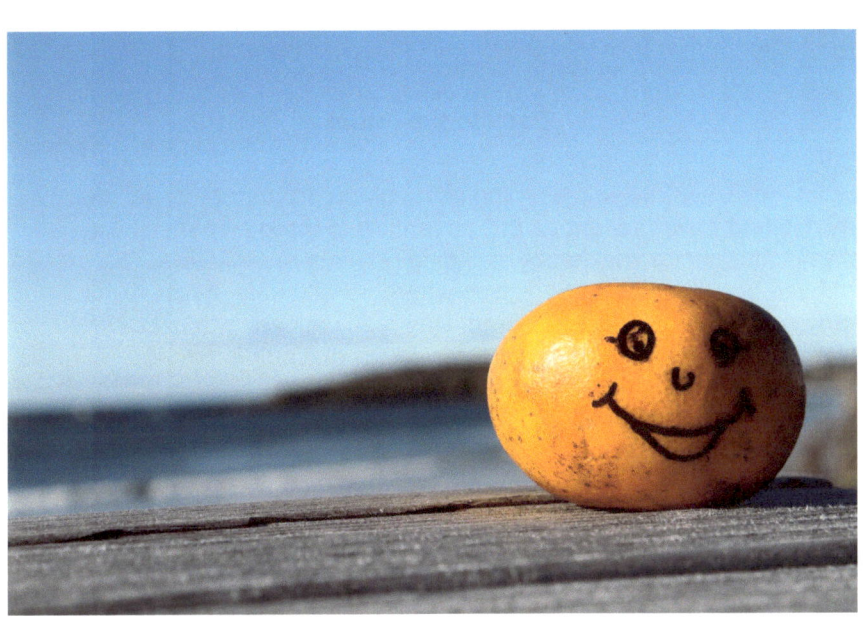

Back to the future

Grant the Grapefruit was learning so much on his journey of self discovery. He had never set out on this adventure to discover himself. He had always thought he was happy swinging on his grapefruit tree. The grapefruit tree was what he knew, it was where he was safe, it was his ordinary life, his comfort zone. If Grant was really honest with himself he never knew anything else existed outside of that comfort zone.

There were times on his journey that Grant had regretted his decision to sit on the banister near a back pack. At other times he was elated by the new discoveries he was making. He was beginning to realise that that is the thing with comfort zones, you never know that you are in one until you make a snap tiny decision and catapult your life in a whole new direction.

Since capturing a brief feeling of his inner grapefruit while resting at Curio Bay, Grant was beginning to realise that he had never really known what true happiness was until then. Now that he had experienced that feeling he wanted to continue to experience it but he wasn't sure how? He began to wonder if grasping at the feeling and trying to cage it like a bird was the wrong method. He wondered how he had managed to get this far in his grapefruit life without realising what true happiness was.
 He began to wonder about his future and what it would hold, where he would go and what would happen to him.

In the mental muddle that was now his mind, which was trying to piece together the segments that made him whole, he nearly forgot to look around him at where he was in the present moment. If it wasn't for a jolt from the mini bus as it went over a bump in the road he would have missed the most beautiful mirror-like glacier lake! Thankfully, the jolt brought Grant back to the present moment and as he became aware of the scenery around him, he suddenly realised that the present moment is the only place that he would have any chance of experiencing that wonderful inner joy again. He was thankful for his rude awakening from his thoughts and made a mental note to himself to ensure that he recognised the next time he was drifting into his mind, or drifting too far into the past or future and bring himself back to the here and now. I mean, who knows what he could have missed if it wasn't for a little jolt on his journey which brought him back to reality and the present moment.

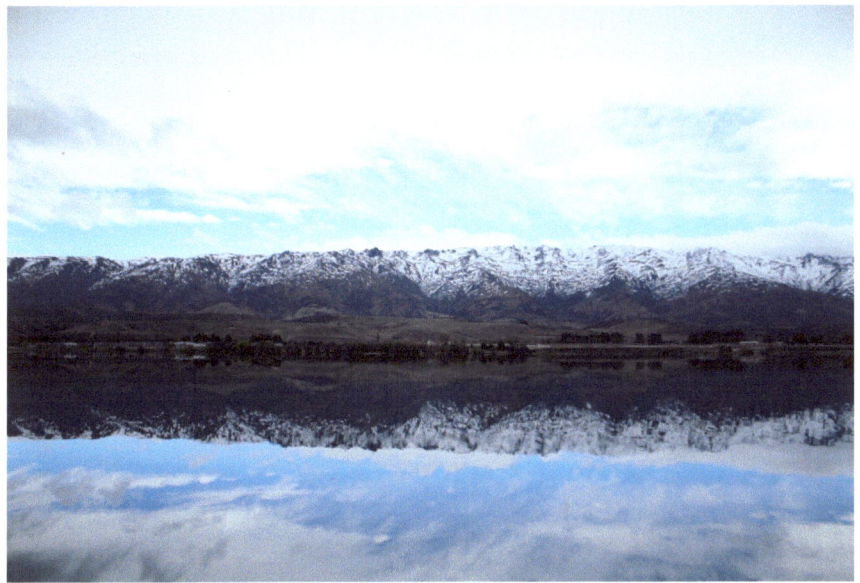

Lifes complications

As the mini bus came to a holt Grant realised he had been sleeping soundly for some time. He had managed to get some much needed rest and he hoped that he had not been drooling grapefruit juice from his mouth as he had been sleeping!

As Grant looked around himself he discovered he was surrounded by beautiful panoramic mountain scenery which took his breath away. Amongst the towering mountain ranges, all competing for skyline space, one stood tall and proud with its illusive peak disappearing into the clouds. Mount Cook, breathed one of Grants travelling companions. On listening closely Grant discovered that Mount Cook is so aloof that he rarely makes an appearance below cloud level.

Now that Grant was becoming a more avid and confident explorer he settled himself in his back pack for the first hike at the Mount Cook National Park ranges. He was happily bouncing around to the rhythmic steps when suddenly there was an unexpected bump and he found himself rolling out of the back pack and landing heavily on the hard, cold stones. Bruised and shocked he couldn't remember what happened next, all he could feel was relief that he wasn't left behind and was placed carefully back in his safe back pack.

The next morning Grant could hardly roll! He was so sore and bruised. Feeling slightly sulky that he would have to take a day off from his adventures and spend it on his own Grant watched as his fellow trek mates got ready to go for another climb. Grant rolled slowly and miserably to a pathway which wound itself towards the mountains wincing with every complete rotation he made.

As he made his way along the path he began to realise that this was actually more fun than he thought it was going to be. He was gently rolling through the narrow paths at his own little pace and he could hear the birds singing and admire the beautiful scenery. He could take his own time, steer himself which ever way he chose to and he began to feel an overwhelming sense of freedom.

Just as he was rounding the corner of the hut, he was honoured to be able to view Mount Cook in all his glory in the morning sun with just a wisp of cloud gently contouring the peak. Grant realised that what sometimes seems at first a painful disaster can actually turn out to be a blessing in disguise.

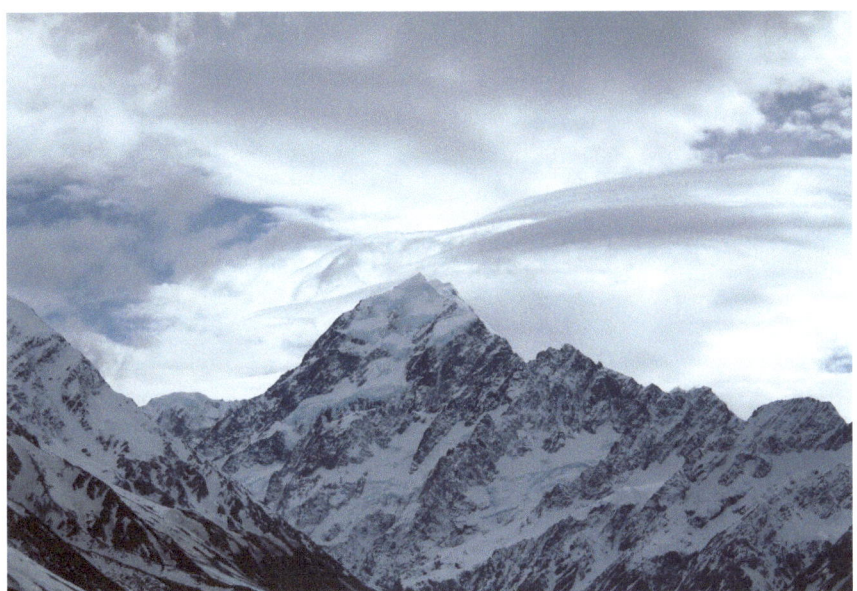

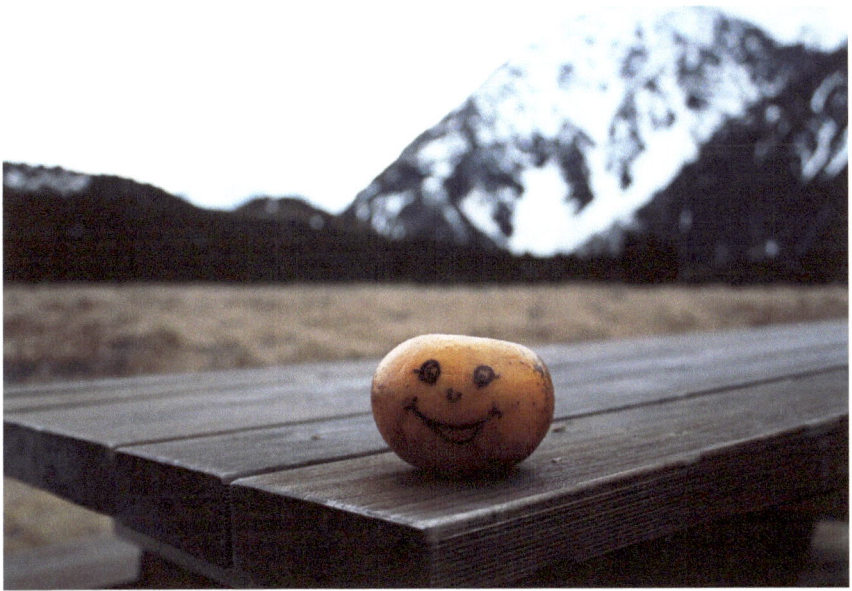

Fear and fame

Being a grapefruit Grant had never watched TV, he had he been to the cinema or seen a film.

From his tree Grant could watch the same patch of garden. Some might think that this would be boring, but Grant had always enjoyed the stillness. He enjoyed the rocking motion of the warm summers breeze and watching the birds dance through the grass and flowers. The back pack he now spent much of his time in reminded him of that same comforting motion but it didn't have the same view. He would be mostly in darkness until he reached his destination, then the views were definitely worth the wait.

Grant recalled a time when he had no dreams, no wishes, no aspirations. He remembered thinking he was content to be like all the other grapefruits on the tree, doing what grapefruits do and not rocking the branches too much because there was always a risk he may fall too soon. Grant started to think about fear, and how that fear of falling had kept him safe in the tree. It had also kept him from experiencing all the wild and wonderful things that the world had to offer. It had kept him from living! He suddenly felt a deep sympathy for the grapefruit friends that he had left behind and wondered if, on his return, they would believe his adventures. He began to wonder if he could return, and realised that sometimes you get so far down a path that there really is no going back, there is only forwards.

Aspirations, dreams, wishes, adventure and courage have done a great many things together, they are a formable team. Grant was honoured as he listened to the discussions going on outside the darkness of his back pack. He knew that he had arrived somewhere of some significance. He heard the words, "Lord of the Rings" and "Twin Towers".

As he was pulled from his back pack another amazing panoramic mountain view was before him. What Grant did not know was that this view was one which had been seen by millions of people world wide. He had no idea how significant the small mound he was resting on was. All he knew was what he saw was pretty special in its own right.

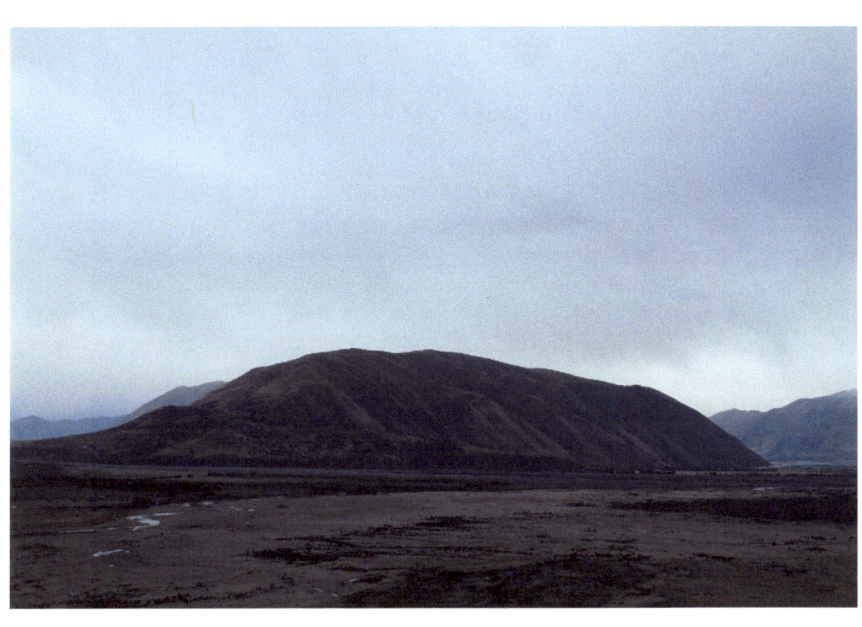

The best is yet to come

Grant was beginning to realise what the saying "life is a journey" really means. Every step, every decision and every realisation that he was having on his adventure was leading to more experiences, more decisions and more realisations unfolding before him.

After finally arriving at Mount Somers and beginning the hike to Woodshed Creek he was in awe at the many snow topped mountains that lay before him. He was beginning to understand that every challenge in life is a like climbing a mountain. It takes a lot of effort and hard work to climb it but the view at the top is worth it!

He was also beginning to realise that once you get to the top of your mountain it gives you the opportunity too see things in a whole new perspective. At the top of your mountain, you are at your peak and you are rewarded for your hard work with the ability to be able to reflect and to look at things from a different perspective. Climbing the biggest mountain means that you can see the smaller ones as less of a challenge. They are not as intimidating. Would it not make sense to rest a while here and take in your surroundings?

This is exactly what Grant did. He watched as his fellow trek mates took photographs so that they could capture and recall the memories of this amazing experience. He began to see how a photograph can be used as a tool for meditation. You sit comfortably and look at the photograph and study it, relax your jaw and face, they do not need to be tense for you to take in all that the photograph has to offer. You can imagine walking down to the hut following the gently winding path, whilst at the same time not rushing and taking a moment to enjoy the feel of the softness of the grass below your feet, how it springs back with every step. You have worked hard on your journey and you need to take a moment to take in the view....then you can reassess and continue walking with a renewed sense of calm, peace and contentment.

At this point Grant realised that what he thought was the top and the end of the journey was, in fact, only a rest point along the way. The best was yet to come.

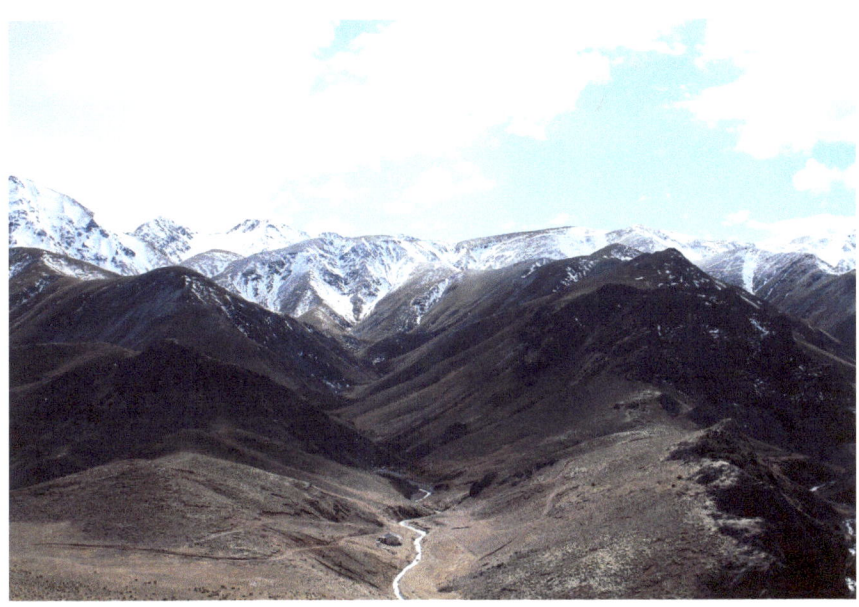

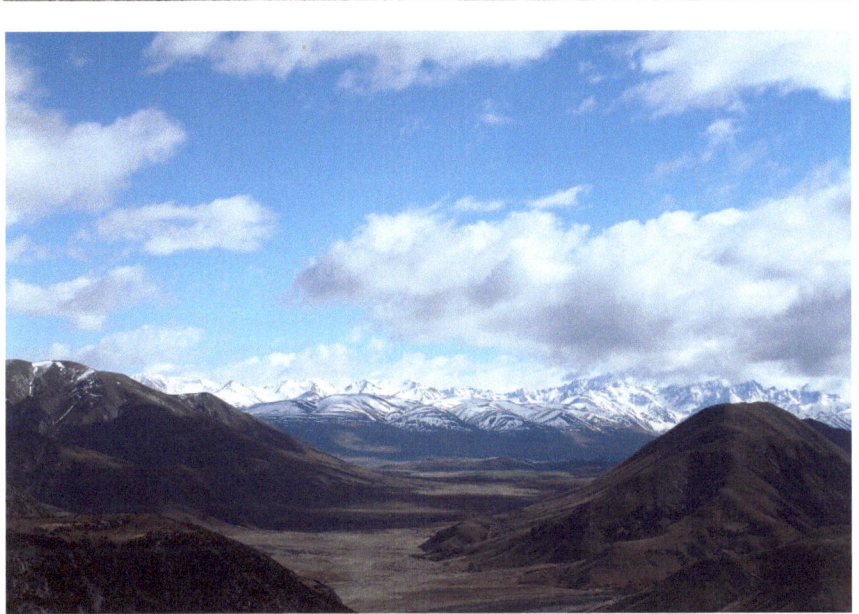

Persistence, determination and why?

Have you ever had one of those challenging times where you have started walking down a path, and you realise that it's getting harder and harder? You tell yourself that it's nearly over, just round this corner and you will be there, you **WILL** get to your destination. You get round the corner and there is another corner waiting for you and your **STILL** not there? It's okay, you tell yourself, you're nearly there, it's nearly over, just round this next corner.....

That is the feeling that Grant the Grapefruit was beginning to get. He thought that he had got to the top of the mountain and he was so wrong. He was beginning to feel completely out of control of this journey now, like he was on the downward ride on the rollercoaster with no way to slow it down or stop it. He knew where he was going, Woodshed Creek. He knew in every segment of his being that he would get there. He just didn't know when, how and what else lay before him. So what do you do when you are in this situation? When you are exhausted and you know that you have to keep going? Motivation is running low and all you really want to do is sit down and cry declaring "Why me?" at the sky.

You have to ask yourself if that would do you any good!

Grant knew that he had two choices, to keep going or to turn back. He decided that he would have to accept that he was not always in control of everything that is happening in his life. Grant decided to trust that he would eventually get to his destination. Grant realised that there is always the option to turn back but then if you look at how far you have come that would be pointless. Sometimes there really is no option but to keep going forwards. Sometimes we can't go back, we have to go forwards or what's the point?

There is an acceptance that whatever is going to happen will happen anyway so you can either: go with it, look around you and try to take as much positive as you can from the ride. Or you can fight it, and cry and whinge and get upset every step of the way. Either way, you are going to have to complete this task. You made the choice to be here and to keep going. It really is up to you how you choose to think and feel about it.

Grant eventually made the decision to stop focusing on the negative. He took some deep breaths and some time to live in the reality of the journey. He looked around him and he realised that whilst he was mentally arguing with himself he had climbed higher than he had ever been in his grapefruit life, and that the views at the top were truly amazing!

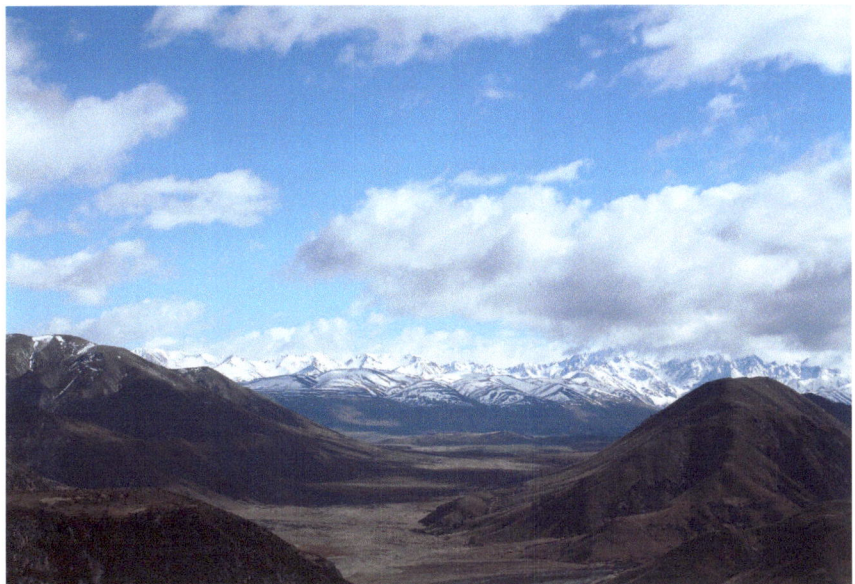

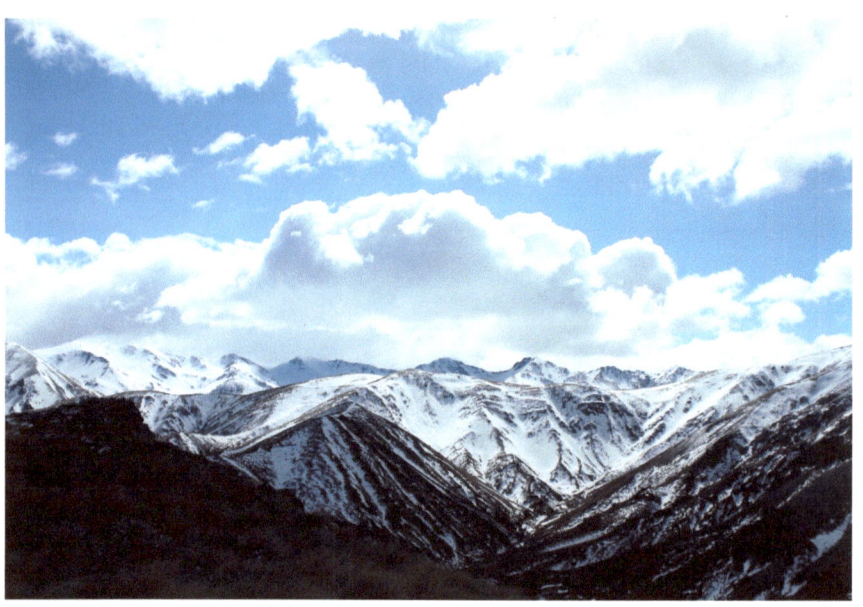

Sharing your experiences

Sometimes you make new friends in the strangest of places.

The long trek to Woodshed Creek Hut left Grant utterly exhausted but oddly elated. As he sat on the worn wooden steps of the hut, he began to feel the presence of someone watching him. From the corner of his smudged eye he could see a beautiful but quite large Kia bird perched on the bannister of the balcony not far from him.

For some time they sat, the two weary travellers, and weighed each other up, not sure whether to trust each other. Grant was wondering whether Kia birds liked grapefruits and was hoping that the bird wasn't sizing him up for a meal.

Finally, Grant started to stiffen up and decided to have a look around and to his surprise his new friend followed him without a sound. They sat by the stream together, not speaking but communicating without words. The land was so peaceful and contentment filled our little adventurous grapefruit. He was so grateful he had someone to share it with.

Grant decided to call the bird, Bob the Kia because the bird would sit and bob his head up and down. Bob seemed just as happy to have company as Grant did. Bob watched his guests silently and with great interest. This is the first time Grant had met another living thing that he did not know how to communicate with and he found he was closely watching Bob, watching him.

Meeting Bob allowed Grant to realise the power of the unspoken word. Sometimes you do not need to say anything. Sometimes all you need is a polite <u>Bob</u> in a stranger's direction to acknowledge that your paths have crossed for a brief moment in time. That your journeys ran alongside each other, just for a moment.

In the silence by the stream Grant realised that although he had only just met Bob, and they did not speak the same language, they were sharing the same experience. Grant began to realise that someone else's reality can be shared in a variety of ways and not all of those are spoken.

Can you spot Grant from Bob's eye view in the photograph below?

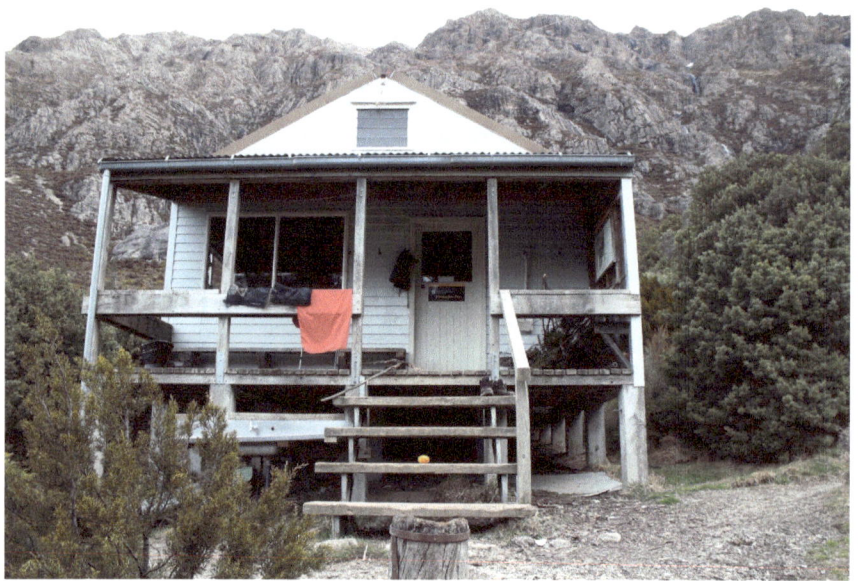

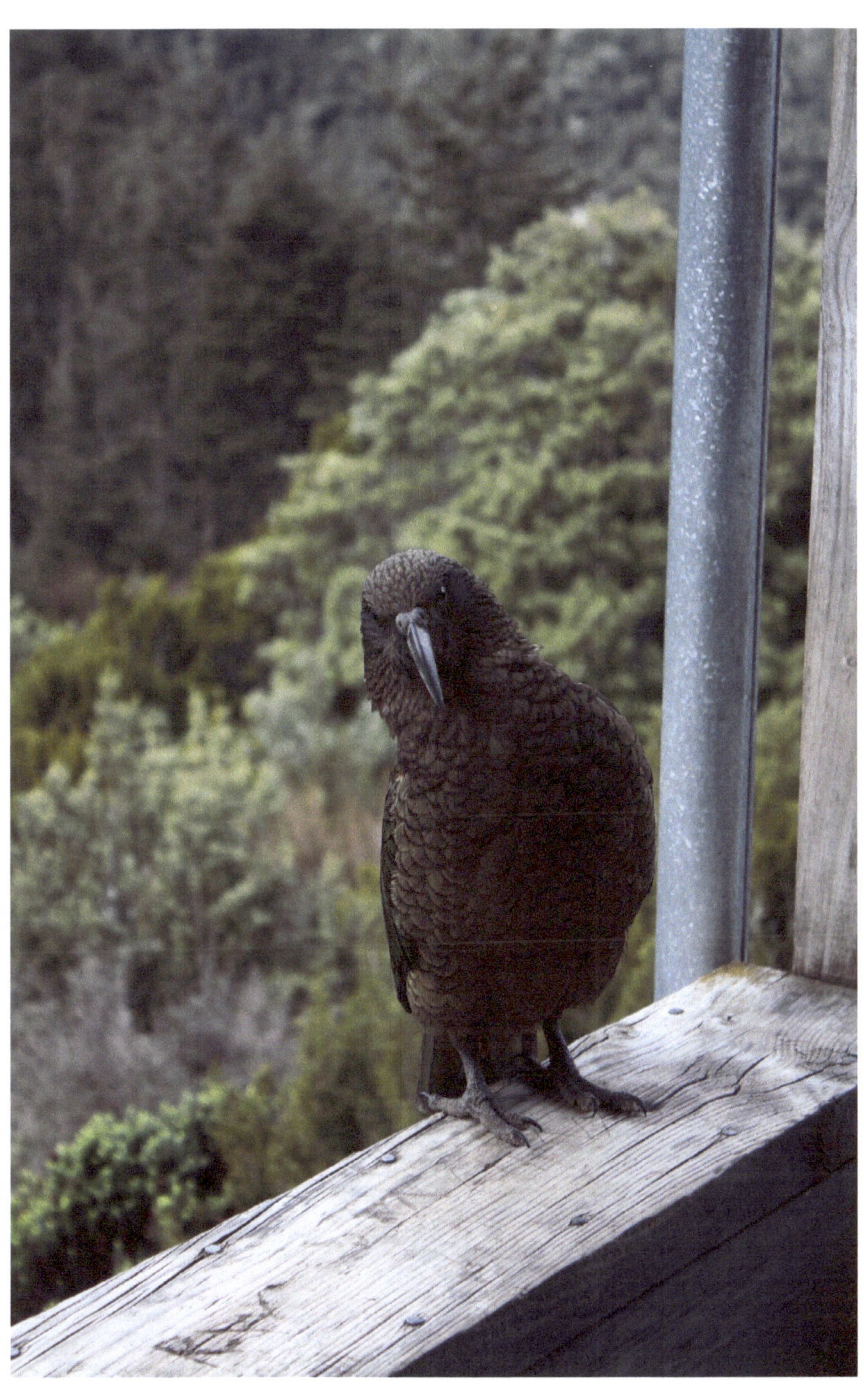

An unexpected twist

Have you ever had a day where you are quite happily getting on with life? You finally feel that you have everything all worked out and planned. You have all the instructions and you know exactly what you are doing and where you are going. Why is it that as soon as you feel like this life has a habit of throwing you a curve ball?

Grant decided that it was to keep him on his toes....if he had any.

After a good nights sleep, Grant opened his eyes and took a peek outside. His eyes then opened even wider. The ground was covered in a thick blanket of white, soft, snow. Grant had never seen snow before and he was really excited. This was the icing on the cake. It was the final trek of his journey and he was happily bouncing from snow drift to snow drift seemingly ignoring the coldness that crept through his thick protective peel.

It was at this moment that Grant's positivity was to be tested. After three hours of playing in the snow he began to get tired and cold and started to wonder if he would ever finish this mammoth journey. He thought he would have been there by now and was beginning to realise that he may have completely underestimated the final stretch of this trek. He was also beginning to realise why it was called a trek! The more tired and weary Grant got, the more upset and negative he felt.

If Grant had realised that the trek would be like this he may not have even started it in the first place!

Grant was so grateful for the whole experience this adventure had offered him, but right now he was bruised, exhausted and had never felt this worn out in his entire life. He had also never felt more alive.

Grant started to realise that the demons he was wrestling with were his own. The journey itself, every experience that he was having and had had along the way, was interpreted and translated by him. He could choose whether to follow his thinking down a negative path, which was an easy route at the moment when he was tired and drained. Or he could choose to change his thoughts and think about how lucky he was to have this experience, to actually see snow, feel snow and view the mountains in a completely different way to how he had seen them the day before. I mean how many grapefruits can say they have had THAT experience?

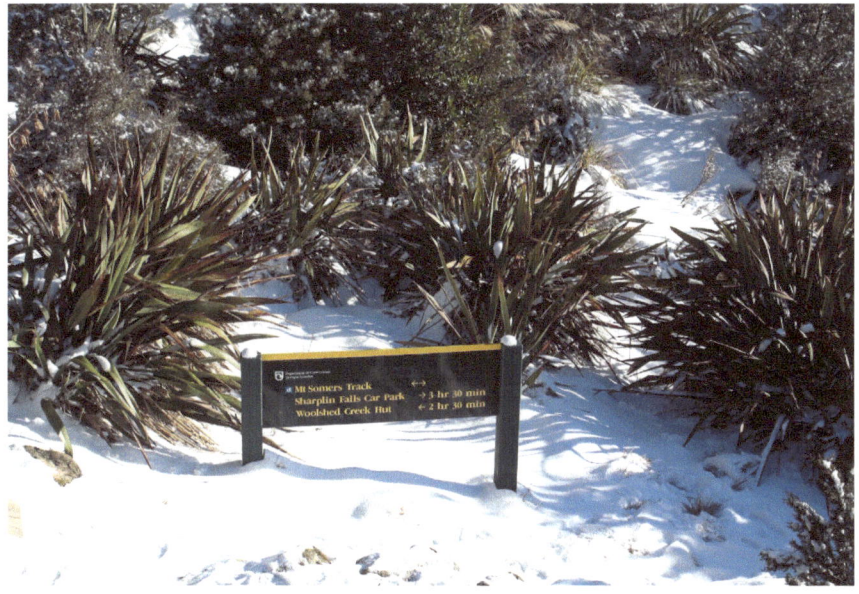

How many times have you looked up?

Being a grapefruit Grant spent most of his time looking up, except of course when he was on a tree. Grant was beginning to learn about perspective. If you look down at something from a high point it can look completely different if you are at the lowest point looking up. This seemed to reflect how Grant was feeling about the final stretch of his adventure. If he changed his perspective a little bit the challenges he faced could look completely different.

Many people are provided the opportunity to look at things from a different perspective throughout their own lives. In fact, you are provided with this opportunity every time you interact with another human being. Each person is living their life from their own personal perspective and that means they are experiencing it in a different way to another person. Grant had begun to realise that your personal interpretation of events was mainly based on your own belief system, your background and the understanding and meaning you place on the events. Through every interaction we have we can choose to look at life from a different perspective.

When Grant was sat comfortably high up in his back pack he would experience the journey from a different perspective to if he was rolling along on a ground level.

How many times have you actually stopped to look up when walking somewhere? On your simple daily journey to work looked up instead of down? What new things would you see and experience that you haven't noticed before?

As Grant stopped to rest and admire the view of the snow covered plants, he looked up. He suddenly experienced a completely different perspective of his surroundings and realised, with joy, that he was resting underneath his own personal waterfall!

Sometimes if you take the opportunity to look at things from a different perspective it can make life seem a whole lot more beautiful!

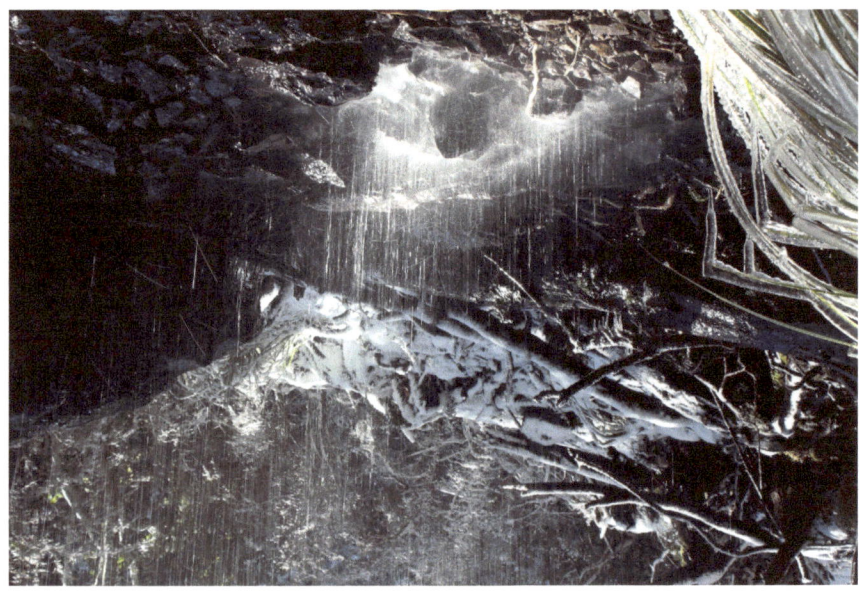

Reality check

Grant was nearing the end of his adventure he could feel it, taste it, sense it. The trek had been exhausting yet enlightening and he was suddenly feeling more motivated knowing the end was in sight. He also felt quite sad that his adventures were coming to a close.

While sat on the rocks having a well earned rest he watched as his human companions were taking photographs of a small waterfall. Two photographs were taken of the same waterfall, from the same place, with the same camera. The only difference between the photographs was the amount of light which was let into the camera. Grant could see on the screen at the back of the camera that the two photographs created a different view of the same thing. In one the water droplets had been frozen in time and were seen as individual splashes. The other photograph showed the movement of the water, blurring its way to join the stream. Yet these two images were of the same thing?

To Grant's grapefruit eyes it seemed like magic...two people could look at the same thing and see it differently!?

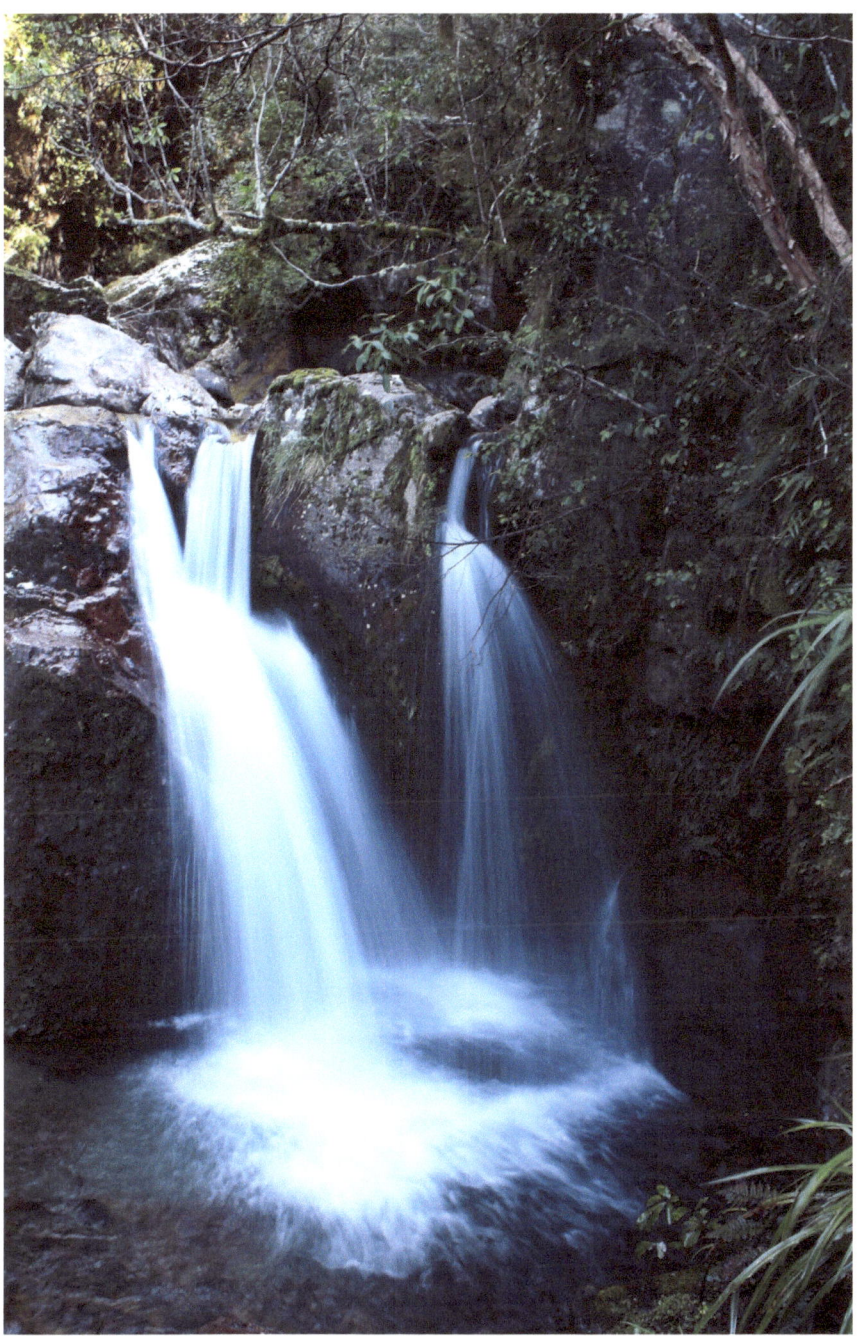

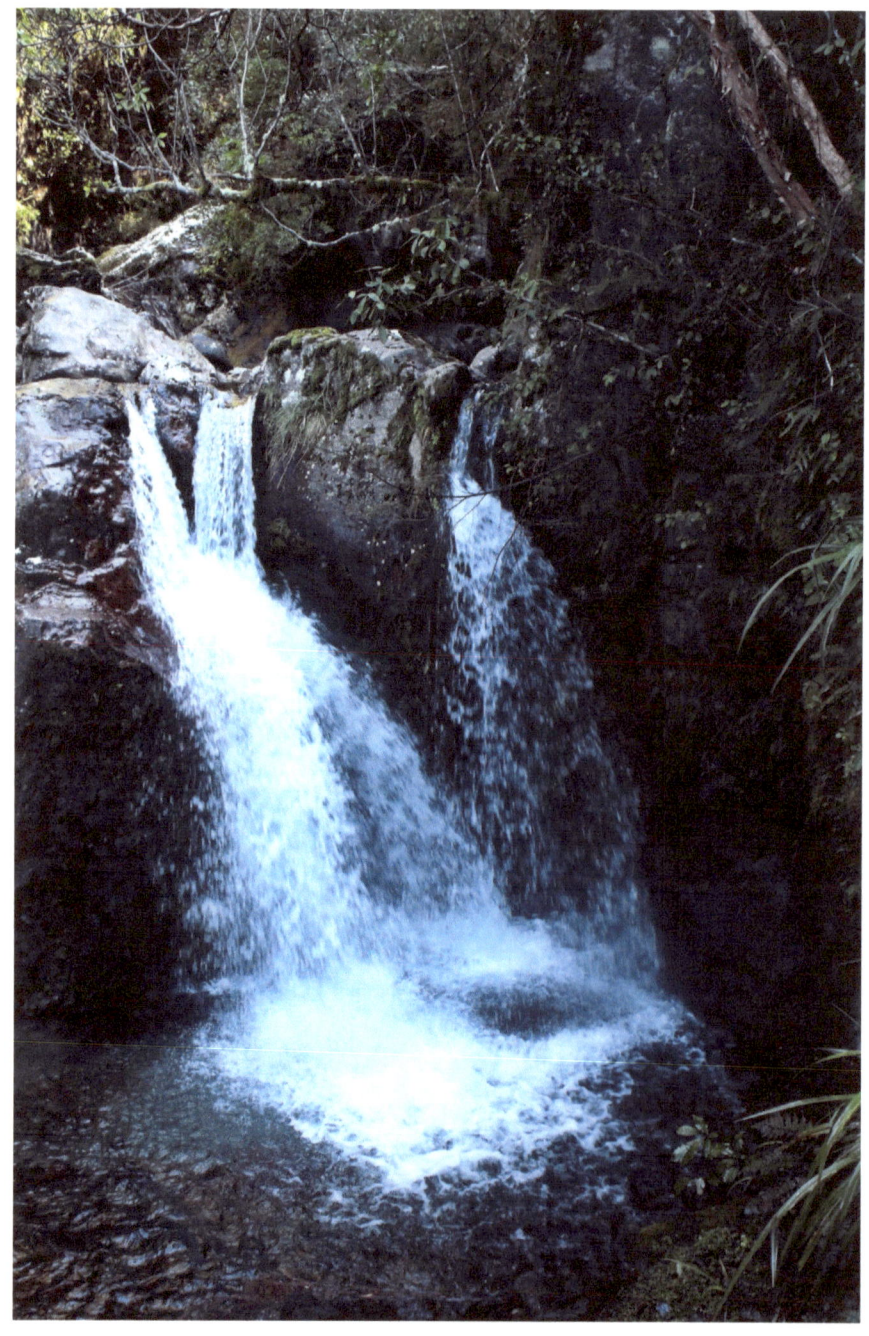

The journeys end

Grant wearily snuggled into a new, larger backpack. He was tired, exhausted but strangely more content than he had ever felt in his life.

Grant's journey had come to an end. There was a feeling of sadness as well mixed with anticipation of what was to come now.

As Grant reflected on the past few weeks and all the things that he had learnt on his adventure he began to question whether our journeys in life ever really end. As one journey ends, a new one begins, because that is the nature of life. It is a cycle and whether you are ready for it or not it will continue to turn taking you with it.

I hope that you have enjoyed following Grant's adventures through New Zealand. Hopefully Grant's bravery and insights have inspired you to add a little grapefruit magic to your day.

Life is a cycle...the end of one set of adventures is the start of another.

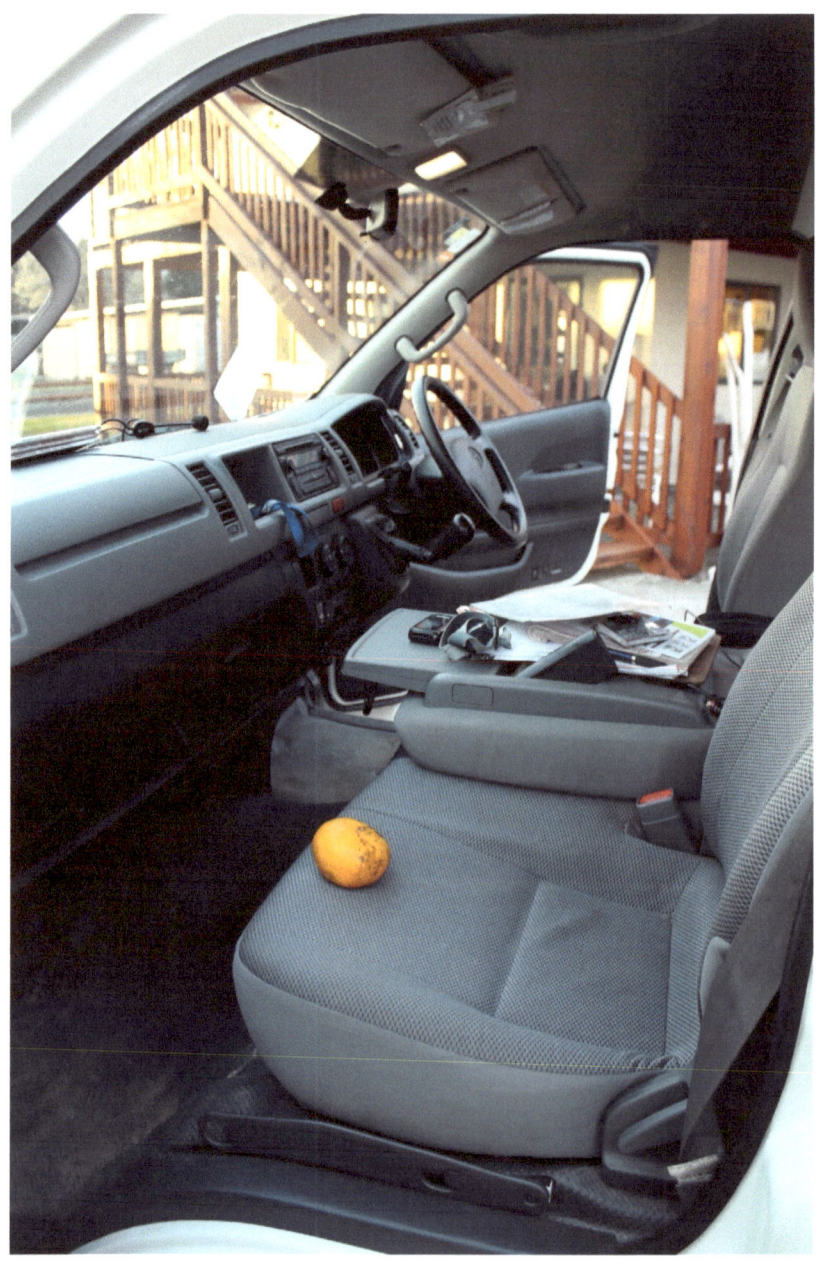

www.ingramcontent.com/pod-product-compliance
Lightning Source LLC
Chambersburg PA
CBHW040922180526
45159CB00002BA/576